LET US (OR THE INVOCATION OF SMOKE)

Shehzar Doja is Founder/Editor-in-Chief of *The Luxembourg Review* and Poetry Reviews Editor at *Gutter*. His poetry and translations have appeared in *New Welsh Review, Pratik, Modern Poetry in Translation, Voice and Verses, Ceremony, Poems from the Edge of Extinction, Gutter, The Centenary Collection for Edwin Morgan, Fundstücke-Trouvailles* and more. His poetry collection *-Drift-* was published by UPL/Monsoon Letters in 2016 and he recently co-edited *I am a Rohingya: Poetry from the Camps and Beyond* (Arc, 2019)with James Byrne which was the recipient of Poetry Book Society's inaugural 'World Choice' award.

Also by Shehzar Doja

I am a Rohingya [w/ James Byrne]   (Arc, 2021)

Drift   (The University Press Limited, 2016)

Let Us (or the Invocation of Smoke)

Shehzar Doja

Broken Sleep Books

ISBN: 978-1-915760-08-1

Cover designed by Aaron Kent

Edited & Typeset by Aaron Kent

Broken Sleep Books Ltd   Broken Sleep Books Ltd
Rhydwen   Fair View
Talgarreg   St Georges Road
Ceredigion   Cornwall
SA44 4HB   PL26 7YH

Contents

Let us sing without voices

When the tune settles
 in bereavement with scalps,

hide— the split fragmentation in
sense, settling interludes to pasture.

Find voice— its shadow is heavy
   and malnourished but still
among the living inhaling a salary of smoke.

When the voice finds itself
again— sing, of the rapture— that myna bird

 that heralds the confluence of sedimentary and vestal rain.
Descend the octave— doldrums, stairs,

perplexing sin to laborious astronomy,
  let monsoon scribe its intent to ink

 vestiges of pomegranate seeded songs
scrying the waves of diminishing voices

the Kal-Boishaki[1] reign masks
no restraint and foliages— to sing without voice.

---

1   Cyclonic pre-monsoon storms.

Let us reposition the stars

Leave the positioning to the stars
We'll carve our own
in pumpkins and lend oracles
a retaliation of conscripts

Let soldiers march through
The *ides* are upon us now
Tangerine led orifice
smelting sulphur from melted wax

Adonis speaks of Beirut
and Myanmar is left unsung
in the ballads of Dylan, B
land of gentry ore and sea passage

A wake without bodies
The children are not playing -and-seek
Reiteration of shelled fingernails
from 'neath the grave

sequence of bridged kaleidoscopes
coloured blind in candy land
Orange juiced perspective
with congenital breakfast in

They say dreams are crescent
they are shaped by the curvature of whips
caressing skin against the back
drip of sin seizing corners

Well, come all, concede all, seed all
After Master Eugenic's race— coronary or
collateral— well done after
all

If there really was a serpent in the ground
maybe we should have noticed
Tilled the garden more,
Home made bogs for marching boots.

Let us begin

Let us begin again
                Let us be Djinn again

in that primordial amniotic
             we never were
 when we were
given breath — our bodies were
already coloured
by fractal light — but we could not see
 the separation by dust we conformed
into

Let us think for a while

 The us as separating threads
The us only available
                with

mirrors and the yous that existed
 but could no longer weigh the
infinity of its own and so
redacted itself as smoke.

Will we begin again as suffering
 no longer in the conquest

of that cyclical bog
adorning us —
Let me build a mosque and yous occupy this
sensate less ness encroaching the solitude with
distant|distant   heaves

Let us begin again —
Embryonic or static ?
What space does
smoke occupy ?

Let us be char

Let infinity loop in eights
               'till it falls on its own
Wait— horizon (tal)
Its proxy slants— comes be
                  fore the sequence
Let us search its ellipses
Take char for fidget spins
'till colours swallow
a dervish dancing into their own *naf^2*

                    Create -Space- as
          much   as a division
                    (Let us) imagine

2   Ego

Let us praise

—Orange trombones
        parry tunes

collected
            debris— diagetic OST
        injections of mould that
           phosphor the

           collective and leave(s)
    the
         abstract
                   fumes— wade
        for a moment whilst
        the sun

        dusks
         this corridor

                        Coronate in
                        suspended caskets

let us think inside this box
let us not

the dislodged spaces

Let us

re—|tire|
now

the genome
of   GO/D

 calligraphy of stolen
          suspension
        &

Let the periphery translate
smoke.
          The periphery is sodded on.
The periphery is an ensemble cast
                    off
                        another

Can you let us… ↓   *here ?…↓*
remember the line(s)
what for?

Let us relive the outline
        —of static, forget the token
          anomalies of script. There
                is always the next breath

    to look forward to
                        to lean against coughing

                                        the   dry
cough off

                                Distil   the
                          roaming air

Retire in supplication
washed hands
watched time
piece on satiated
rest. Be still now
roaming heir
Greet the transient—
                    scrapping tomorrows

Let us break

Letters break away in fumes/ bask in/congruity/ and the silted
fingers/still replenish/still
nest/stubborn as wading air/watered supplication/threads plastered
over un/becoming of/to be/coming home/to find the drifting/smoke
lodged and heav/y rest now?/ break—
pause the passage/ways are ab/rupture the stars with skin and
smoke/Dim the humming myna bird/ nurtures the advent of/
Eye may/be/spoke/the sweltered/canvas/and let/the reprieve drip
in/sensate
Let us break/ our fast/ this evening/ turn the coal/ water / our
vapoured lungs/ script the periphery/
Prosper/us / in gold/in roam/and haze

Let Us in

The smoke (too quick to -   curates its scurried
transience) : Across the bound/less lines –roam.
Make peace and fall/ low the line of A/adam (PBUH)

the world mad/e flesh: (electric, of new - smokeless
flesh, a/new, sizzled between truth and a silent s)
: Ob/serve the un/claimed passage(s)
of song (and be silence)

I do

not understand -

this verse,

Let us in –

Read:
The cast is silent.
The cast observes.
 An erasured silence is cast upon the edge( ) of the Word.

Let us find voice, and skin, and hide

(already hidden)

Let us see/quest/err

(is it not the same?)

Let us profit

(there is no prophet among us)

Let us exist with /in –

(parenthesis)

Let us reposition

(s)crying)

Let us in/finite

                        (charred)

Let us not be the

                        (sieved)

Let us drift

                    (as/ in smoke   …

back

)

Acknowledgements

A big thank you to my MLitt and DFA cohort and department at the University of Glasgow, that helped me work on and edit the poems over the years and a special acknowledgement in particular to my supervisor Dr Colin Herd, whose patience, support and enthusiasm over the years on the concept helped launch Shisha Poetics into the world.

A special acknowledgement to Iain Morrison and Fruitmarket Gallery (Edinburgh) for helping launch Shisha Poetics in its artistic incarnation via the exhibition.

Poems from this Anthology have previously been published in:

The Best Asian Poetry 2021 Anthology (KITAAB) ed: Sudeep Sen
~ Let us sing without voices
~ Let us break

Poetry Wales 57.2
~ Let us Begin

Four Letter Words anthology ed: Nicky Melville
~Let us praise   the dislodged spaces

LAY OUT YOUR UNREST

www.ingramcontent.com/pod-product-compliance
Lightning Source LLC
Chambersburg PA
CBHW031637040426
42452CB00007B/858